Turn Your Art into Cash

Branding & Marketing Your Creative Product

Judi Moreo

Las Vegas, Nevada 89120
United States of America

Cover design and typesetting: Jake Naylor

ISBN-13: 978-0-9882307-9-8

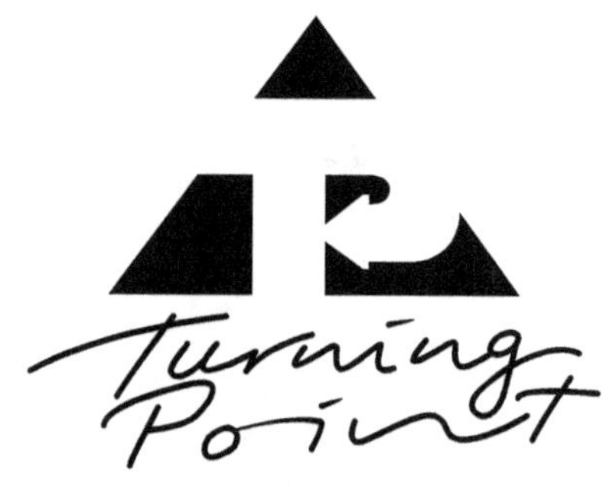

3315 E. Russell Road, Ste. A4-404
Las Vegas, Nevada 89105
(702) 283-4567

Published in the United States of America

Disclaimer

This book is designed to provide information on promoting and selling art. It is sold with the understanding that the publisher and author are not engaged in rendering legal, accounting or other professional services. If legal or other expert assistance is required, the services of a competent professional should be sought.

It is not the purpose of this book to reprint all the information that is otherwise available to artists, but instead to complement, amplify, and supplement other texts.

You are urged to read all the available material, learn as much as possible about marketing your art, and tailor the information to your individual needs.

Every effort has been made to make this book as complete and as accurate as possible. However, there may be mistakes, both typographical and in content. Therefore, this text should be used only as a general guide and not as the ultimate source of marketing and selling your art. Furthermore, this book contains information that is current only up to the printing date.

The purpose of this book is to encourage and educate. The author and Turning Point International shall have neither liability nor responsibility to any person or entity with respect to any loss or damage caused, or alleged to have been caused, directly or indirectly, by the information contained in this book.

If you do not wish to be bound by the above, you may return this book to the publisher with your receipt for a full refund.

Judi Moreo, CSP

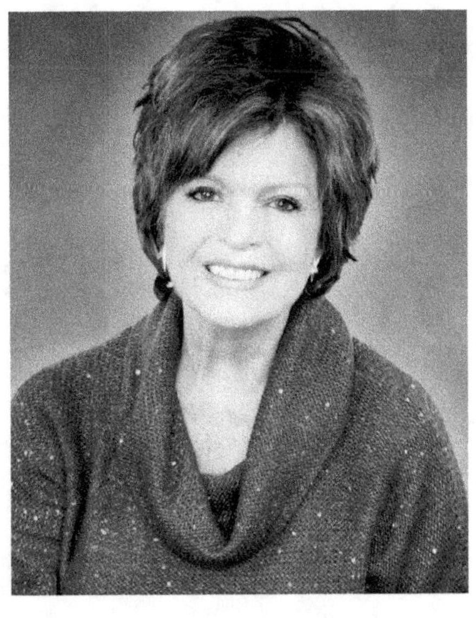

Judi Moreo is an artist, a certified speaking professional, author, publisher of *Choices* magazine, host of *The World of Creativity* television show and a life-long entrepreneur with 40+ years of experience creating brands and building businesses. She has twenty-five years of experience in the media world hosting television and radio shows, working as a journalist, podcasting, and serving as the Group Promotions Manager for the largest media group in Africa. In addition, Judi has produced many of the largest tradeshows in America and was instrumental in bringing the convention industry to Las Vegas.

Judi teaches both watercolor and acrylic painting and does workshops on "Marketing and Branding Your Creative Products."

For information on her classes, workshops, and other books, contact Judi Moreo at (702) 283-4567, judi@judimoreo.com or www.judimoreoartist.com.

Table of Contents

Section 1

Branding

Where I grew up in South Texas, when people talked about branding, they were talking about permanently marking their animals by way of heat to indicate ownership of those animals. If our cows got onto the open range and somehow got mixed in with your cows, that brand would tell us which cows were ours and which ones were yours.

Today, branding is a marketing term meaning making identifiable a name, logo, slogan, and/or a design scheme with a product or service. As an artist, you want people to readily be able to tell your art from someone else's art. So, it is important for you to create a brand... for your art and for yourself. You do this by distinguishing your name, your art, your story, your purpose and your quality. But, how do you do this?

Start with a target audience. Who do you want to buy your art? Who do you want to support you? Who do you want to promote you? Where do these people live? How can you make them aware of you?

Get involved in your art community. Display your art everywhere you think your possible buyers will be...

galleries, art shows, restaurants, city hall, anywhere that you can get someone to let you hang your art. In order to get known, your work must get seen. Put your art on the internet. Display your work on Pinterest, Instagram, Facebook and any other website where you know people will be looking at art. In the resources section of this book, I list hundreds of websites and social media sites where you can sell your art. The audience is out there and it IS possible to sell your art, but you must do the work. You can't just sit on your behind and expect people to discover you.

Your image is a part of your brand. Is the image you have now telling the world that you are a successful artist? I have a photographer friend in Las Vegas who wears a railroad engineers cap everywhere she goes. She was wearing it when I first met her and every time I have seen her since. It fits her personality and thus is a part of her brand. People know who she is imme-diately...even across a crowded room, because they recognize her by the hat.

When I was a child, there was a lady that appeared on the Grand Ole Opry who wore a hat with the sales tag hanging on it. If you are over 30, you probably immediately said, "Minnie Pearl." That's the power of branding.

How will you become memorable? Will you wear red glasses like Sally Jessy Raphael used to do on all of her television show appearances? Or, clothing covered in bling like Liberace? Or, perhaps you have a great pair of jeans that have paint smears artfully positioned on them? Think about what you can do to stand out from the others. You don't want to just show up. You want to be different in a very memorable way.

Your brand includes your price range. You have to determine whether you will be an artist who sells your paintings at a low, medium, or high price range. Will you paint in only one medium? Will you only paint one specific subject matter i.e. flowers, African animals, abstracts, etc. Will you paint only in certain colors? Or, have a specific item like a red umbrella or a black cat in every painting? What space do you want to own in people's minds? How do you want to be known? Who do you want to know you?

You must identify and understand your target market. If you don't know who is going to buy your art, how will you produce what they will buy? The more you know about your market, the closer you can get to making art that is relevant to your buyers. After all, you are not trying to sell just one painting to one person. You are wanting to create clients...people who want to buy painting after painting or art piece after art piece. Hopefully, they will become collectors of your art.

It is imperative that you understand who is buying your art. Many clients are buyers who want to make an impression on their friends. They want others to know they are successful and can afford to buy expensive paintings. They aren't thinking about whether that painting matches their couch or covers a blank space on their wall. Of course, there are people who buy paintings for those reasons and you have to know which you are dealing with. These people are usually not as apt to invest higher amounts of money in their paintings. But, if this is your customer, you may sell more paintings at a lower price point. Usually, the scarcer your paintings are, the higher the price point.

My business partner and I were bidding a training job to a large corporation whose company name was the scientific name of a particular butterfly. They were just moving into new offices and I commented that perhaps a few paintings of butterflies by my business partner's mother would go nicely in their offices. The company president became very indignant and explained to me that they had a curator find the very best artist in the world who specialized in butterflies and they had paid an enormous amount of money for their curator collection. He made it very clear that he was not interested in anyone's mother's paintings. Needless to say, I shut up and didn't say anymore at that time. He was so impressed with his collection, he took us into his boardroom to show the collection to us and went into great detail about the paintings and the artist. As it turned out, it was my partner's mother who had painted his entire collection. I debated whether or not I should tell him. Oh, what the heck! I told him. You see, he didn't want paintings by just anyone's mother. He wanted paintings by a well-known branded artist. When he found out my business partner was this famous artist's daughter, he treated us totally differently. Go figure!

Branding

You must be aware that you are selling more than a painting. You are selling emotions. How does your painting make someone feel? Many buyers of art buy because something about that art has touched them. You are selling something intangible. You are selling the story behind the painting. That story may be yours or it may be theirs. We'll get to your story shortly. Right now, let's concentrate on theirs.

The art makes them feel something. Or, it reminds them of something, some place, someone who was special in their lives. It may be they are trying to send a message by the type of art they display on their walls. Are they trying to save wildlife, or is the ecology important to them? Do they wish to show their attention to social responsibility by the pictures of orphaned children they display?

When someone buys your art, they have connected with you. Branding is telling people who you are, what you do, and your purpose for doing it. You want your brand to stand for quality. Your branding is making others aware that you exist. It is your credibility. It is trust. It is created slowly, over time. Consistency and repetition are imperative to branding..

This is where your story comes in. Every painting should have a story. First, give it a name. And then create its story. To do this, think about your art...what makes it different? Why did you paint it? What is the meaning behind it? What are you trying to say with the painting? What inspired you to paint this particular picture? What does it represent? Where were you?

Was it difficult to paint? What challenges did you have to overcome? What emotions were you feeling when you painted it? Were you scared? Were you in love? Were you angry? Ask yourself, who am I touching with the painting and what is important to them? Most people have no clue how an artist works, and they enjoy the glimpse into the process.

People love stories. People buy stories. Stories can be told and handed down through generations. When clients show your paintings to others, they will share your story because it adds dimension to the painting for them.

Don't expect people to understand your painting. It is important that you lead them to an understanding of your desired perception of the painting. Explain to them what you were attempting to convey when you painted the piece. Type up your story and put it on the back of the painting along with the Certificate of Authenticity. Don't make them have to discover it on their own.

Every painting must have a story. And, you must make it known that you want your painting to find its place in a very good home where people will love it and care for it as you have...people who will show it, talk about it, and share its story. It's important they appreciate both the work and you as the artist. This will impact your career because these people will become your advocates.

Art Is a Business

You have spent many hours enhancing your artistic skills, and you are ready to share your work with the world. If you want to make a living with your art, you need to address it as a business instead of a hobby. Starting an art business is very exciting, and there is no better time than now to start an art business because you have the power of the internet to share your art with people all around the world.

The cost of operating an online business is inexpensive, and the traffic that an online business can receive is unimaginable. The more people who see your art, the more likely you are to sell some of your work. And since the cost of selling on the internet is low, you stand to make more profit.

As with all businesses, you need to start with a clear vision for your business.

Your vision is what you would like to achieve. What are your goals? Are you looking to become a full-time artist, hoping to supplement an income, or are you content with this being only a hobby? Each vision will lead you down different paths, so it is important to know where you eventually want to end up.

Where do you want to go? In the story of Alice in Wonderland, you will remember that when Alice got to a fork in the road, the Cheshire Cat was up in a tree observing her. Alice asked the Cat, "Which way should I go?" and the Cat asked her where she was going. When she replied that she didn't really know, the Cat then said, "It doesn't matter which road you take. Any road will get you there." In other words, if you don't know where you are going, how will you know which path to follow?

You need to establish what success looks like to you, as an artist. Is it financial prosperity, recognition for your work or just a feeling of accomplishment? Perhaps you will set a target of a certain number of pieces you will sell every month; plan to participate in a certain number of exhibitions in the next year or enter certain art competitions.

Once you have a clear vision of what you want, you can start setting your goals for getting there. It's important that they be measurable and attainable, so you will know when you get there and can measure your progress along the way.

Your Target Market

It's imperative that you determine who your specific customers are and target them directly. There is an audience for every artist, and it's up to you to identify who is in your target market.

When you can identify the people you need to target, you'll be saving yourself time, energy and money. Not only do you need to recognize who loves your art, but you also need to determine if they can actually afford to buy it.

Once you have established who they are, it is important to find out where they hang out.

- Who are your ideal customers?
- Where do they live?
- What social media sites do they visit the most?
- Are they involved with any groups?
- What online content do they read?
- What blogs or sites do they frequently visit?
- Why would they want to visit your site?
- Are they subscribed to your email list? If not, how can you encourage them to subscribe?

The more specific you are, the better able you will be to make an effective marketing plan.

"*If you hear a voice within you say, 'You cannot paint,' then by all means paint, and that voice will be silenced.*"

– Vincent Van Gogh –

Section 4

Your Marketing Plan

It's time to create your marketing plan so you can get your art in front of the people who matter and make sure that you're hitting your targets. No one else can explain your art to customers better than you, so you should be the one to sell it.

- What type of art will you sell?
- How much art can you create in a year?
- How much will you make the first year? Break this down into months as well.
- How much will your art have to sell for in order to reach the income you desire?
- Where will you sell your art?
- How will you market your art?

The first step is to write out specific objectives. Take some time to decide what you would like to accomplish. It can be one, two or even three different goals. Having a clear vision of what you are working for will make it easier for you to develop a plan.

After you have listed your objectives, write specific actions you will take to achieve these objectives.

Let's say your goal is to sell five paintings this month. Then your plan will look something like this:

1. Create five paintings by a certain date.
2. Upload photos of them on your website by a certain date
3. Write 5 separate blog posts that will tell the story behind each piece of art. (Assign dates to be posted.)
4. Promote the art and blog posts on your social media sites. (Post 4 x per day on all sites)
5. Send an email to your email list by a certain date.

When you have completed your list of actions, check them against your objectives and make sure they are in keeping with your goals. Every action should take you closer to achieving your objective.

Once you have your plan written out, take action. Nothing works until you do. And of course, you should have dates when you will review your plan and assess how you are doing. Are you on track? Did you meet your estimated completion dates for each task? What things should you revise for the future.

"Creativity takes courage."

– Henri Matisse –

Pricing Your Art

Many artists find it difficult to set a price for their art. And, I have to admit, it is confusing. There are so many factors to consider. First, there is how much time you spent creating the piece, the material costs, the costs of your gas, your booth, art show or gallery fees. Then, there are other factors such as your experience, how much you value your time, the quality of your art, what other artists are charging for similar artwork, what your artwork has sold for in the past, how well known you are, and whether or not there is a demand for your work. Some artists even charge by the square inch.

With commissioned paintings, you may want to charge more because commissions can be more work and sometimes the clients can be a real pain. This takes up your time, and time is money. Always get a non-refundable deposit of 50% on a commissioned piece. One artist I know painted a beautiful white horse for a woman and when it was finished, she swore it didn't look exactly like her horse (which it did) and refused to pay for it. You can't afford to spend a great deal of time painting something, only to have the client refuse to pay in the end.

Your prices don't have to be the same everywhere. You may have one price on your website and a different price at a show. However, if your artwork is hanging in a gallery and you are doing a show nearby, you should keep your prices the same as in the gallery.

The bottom line is you must set a price. If your art doesn't sell at that price, lower your prices. If you are selling a lot, try raising your prices. Don't lower your prices to compete with other artists. No two pieces of art are alike and should not be priced alike. You can't compete on price with other artists. They may not mind selling for a small percentage over costs and not understand that art is a business. There's a lot more to running a business than selling one piece of art. You have every right to assign whatever price you feel is the value of your work. No one is obligated to buy it at that price. If they want to offer you a lower price, you feel it is fair and you want to take the offered amount, then do so. I have pieces I will not sell for under a certain amount because of the time and effort I put into painting them as well as my love for the pieces. I won't turn loose of it unless it is so much money that I just can't refuse. Even though people have told me, "You can paint another one," I probably won't.

Purchasing art is a luxury, not a necessity. Every sale is the perception of the customer as to whether or not your work is worth the value of the cash he is willing to pay for it.

Once a person buys one of your paintings, it is of upper most importance for you to keep in touch with that person. Send them a postcard once a month with an announcement of your new paintings, shows, exhibits, or just to say hello. Staying in contact on a regular basis is how you turn one-time buyers into repeat customers.

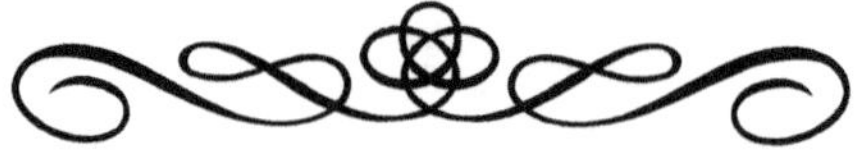

"*Imagination is the beginning
of creation.
You imagine what you desire,
you will what you imagine,
and at last,
you create what you will.*"

- George Bernard Shaw -

Section 6

Artist Bio

People love stories, so it is important for artists to tell their stories via a bio and a headshot on the back of the artwork, even on matted artwork which is not framed.

Tell why you make your art, what inspires or drives you to make it, why people should care, what it signifies or represents, what it communicates, what's unique or special about how you make it, and briefly, what it means to you. Write this in first person, so the buyer knows it came from you. This will form a stronger bond between the art piece, the artist, and the buyer.

Include a picture of yourself on the bio sheet so the customer can recognize that you are the artist. And be sure the picture is up-to-date so you are recognizable.

"You don't take a photograph,
you make it."

— Ansel Adams —

Section 7

Certificate of Authenticity

The Certificate of Authenticity should be placed on the back of matted and framed artwork. This certificate should give information specific to the art pieces such as the Title of the painting, Artist Name, Date of Original, Medium, Size, Value, and the artist signature.

Certificate of Authenticity

ORIGINAL ARTWORK BY JUDI MOREO

This is to certify that the art described on this certificate is an authentic and original work by artist Judi Moreo. A digital master of the work is in the possession of the artist and a "Print on Demand" basis may be used until the close of an edition. All fine art, including reproductions should be protected and kept from direct sunlight, intense heat and humidity.

Title _______________________________   Date Completed _______________________________

Image Size _______________________________   Estimated Value _______________________________

_______________________________________   ___________________

Artist's Signature   Date

www.JudiMoreoArtist.com | (702) 283-4567 | judi@judimoreoartist.com

Recently I have seen these added to the bottom of the Artist Bio or the Story of the Painting making only one document on the back of the artwork.

The Art of Judi Moreo

As long as I have been able to read, I have been fascinated by Africa and African animals. As a child, I would sit in the hallway at my aunt's home, read her National Geographic magazines and dream of the time I would be old enough to go to Africa.

Fortunately, for me, I had the opportunity to live and work in Africa for 8 years and make many trips back to the continent in the years that followed. I have spent countless hours in the bush observing and photographing the animals, the people, and their culture.

I have been enamored by the animals. As I paint them, their personalities emerge. I feel as though I experience their souls. I paint them as realistically as I possibly can as I want the viewer of my paintings to see what I have seen. I hope you will love them as much as I do.

Certificate of Authenticity

ORIGINAL ARTWORK BY JUDI MOREO

This is to certify that the art described on this certificate is an authentic and original work by artist Judi Moreo. A digital master of the work is in the possession of the artist and a "Print on Demand" basis may be used until the close of an edition. All fine art, including reproductions should be protected and kept from direct sunlight, intense heat and humidity.

Title _______________________________   Date Completed _______________________

Image Size __________________________   Estimated Value _______________________

____   _______________
Artist's Signature   Date

www.JudiMoreoArtist.com | (702) 283-4567 | judi@judimoreoartist.com

Promoting Your Art

There are plenty of ways you can promote offline. All it takes is a little bit of planning and persistence.

You want to become the go-to source for advice in your community. That means stepping up and positioning yourself as an expert. Being an expert doesn't mean you have all the answers or that you develop a big ego. Being an expert means you're a leader who cares about and protects your community. So, how can you be seen as an expert? Try doing some of these things:

Get Featured on Podcasts

Find podcasts in your niche and start listening. Which ones do you enjoy the most? Which hosts sound like they'd be a good fit for your personality? If you find several possibilities, write them down so you know who you need to contact.

After you've found a few podcasts, pop onto their websites. Check to see if the host is looking for more guests. If you can't find any information about being a guest, reach out to the host directly. Ask her what her criteria is for choosing guests and see if you fit the bill.

Find Journalist Requests

There are websites where journalists will post about what stories they're working on and request experts to interview. This can be an excellent way to boost your visibility and be seen as an art leader.

Some of these sites, like Help A Reporter Out (www. helpareporterout.com), are free to join. If you want additional features, you may want to purchase a monthly subscription. The reporter's requests are sorted according to niche, making it easy for you to scan for opportunities that are right for you.

When you first start promoting yourself as an expert, you may not get a lot of traction. But keep sharing your knowledge and doors will begin to open for you.

There are many avenues for marketing.... Your website, social media, advertising, events, reviews, articles, tv, radio, newspapers, newsletters, billboards, magazines. Before you start dumping money into any and all of these, be sure your plan is in place. Which one will you do first? How much money will you bring in before you add the second one? Remember if you want to be visible you must make a plan to be out there in front of the same people several times a week. And be sure those people are the right people.. It won't do you any good to reach millions of people, if they are the wrong people. And be sure everything links back to your website.

Build your plan for next year right now. And when I say plan, I mean what you are going to have happen month by month, week by week, day by day. What shows are you going to exhibit in and how are you going to promote your work? How many paintings are you going to complete? What is the subject matter? How are you going to promote them when they are finished?

Give Branded Gifts to Strangers

You can start by carrying promotional gifts with you. These don't have to be huge items. They can be pens, notepads, or coffee mugs with your website address and artist tagline. Then you can pass these items out as you meet people. Give a cashier your promotional postcard or hand a pen to the lady in line behind you at the bank.

Attend Conferences

Grow your artist base by attending conferences in your niche. This will help you form valuable industry relationships, too. Don't try to meet and interact with every single person attending.

Instead, focus on serving others and making genuine connections with a few people. If someone asks what you do, be prepared with a short pitch about your art. If you have promotional items with your art on them, you can pass them out.

Speak at Events

Look around for seminars and networking events that could use a speaker. If you know the event budget is tiny and you want the experience of speaking, offer to do the program for free. You can also ask about making a two-minute pitch about your art at the end, if the event coordinator is agreeable.

If possible, have someone there to record your speech so you can upload it to a video site. This will not only show off your speaking abilities, it also gives you a chance to turn your offline content into an online marketing opportunity.

Not comfortable speaking to groups? Try joining an organization like Toastmasters. Local groups meet monthly so members can improve their speaking skills. If you'd like to speak at events regularly, then this can be a great way to jumpstart your speaking career.

Don't be afraid to talk about your art or promote it to others. Most people look at artists a bit like they look at celebrities. They're fascinated by what you do and curious to know more.

Marketing your art can be fun and rewarding. The more you do it, the easier it gets. But don't forget to take notes about what's working for you and what isn't.

This will help you have plenty of promotion ideas when it's time to promote your next piece!

"Don't think.
Thinking is the enemy of creativity.
It's self-conscious,
and anything self-conscious
is lousy.
You can't try to do things.
You simply must do things."

- Ray Bradbury -

Advertising

Advertising is not something you do just one time. So, don't buy that magazine or tv ad once and wait to see what your return will be. I can tell you right now, it will be zero. You must establish trust with the readers of the magazine or the viewers of the tv show, and it takes seeing your name and your artwork about seven times before anyone buys, so one ad is just throwing your money away.   If you are going to spend money on advertising, establish a budget and advertise month after month. This develops awareness. As an artist, you must build your brand with your audience by consistently exposing your name and your art to the world.

Don't spread your advertising dollar across many media outlets. Dominate one and when you have the finances, add another one. Advertising builds awareness. Consistent advertising over long periods of time creates sales. Be sure that your ads have a headline, an image with a caption, a story (which is your emotional appeal) and a call to action.

The same applies to shows. The typical sale takes seven contacts before a customer makes a purchase. The more times they see your art in advertising, exhibits, galleries, stores, and shows, the closer you are to a sale.

Art purchases are usually an emotional decision. Someone sees your work and loves it, or it reminds them of something or someone. Then their logical thinking kicks in...can they afford it, is it worth the money, how can they justify the purchase. This is where you must be ready to justify the spend by making sure to tell them about the worth of the painting. You are selling emotion, memories, feelings. You are also selling your brand and your notoriety.

"Every artist was first an amateur."

- Ralph Waldo Emerson -

Participating in Art Shows

Your Booth

When you are exhibiting your work at an art show and visitors walk past your booth and look in, you want to have something that intrigues their curiosity enough to make them want to come inside. Display your absolute best pieces of art on the back wall, as that is the wall that is viewed the most. Be sure there is nothing obstructing the view to that wall.

The booth itself should in no way detract from your art. You want to make the booth space inviting and easy to navigate. Don't block the front of your booth with a table or chairs. Create an open layout that allows the visitor to see your artwork without feeling like they are "corralled". Position a small work table for yourself in an area that enables you to view the booth interior yet doesn't obstruct the flow.

Visitors are usually interested in watching someone create artwork. You can position yourself at an easel or work station so that passers-by can see what you are doing.

Ensure there are no electrical cords, protruding table legs, or booth bases in the path where visitors can trip over them. Also, be aware of tablecloths that are too long and dragging on the floor where a visitor might get caught up in it. You don't want someone falling in your space.

Lighting is always an issue in a booth. Focus on lighting your art rather than your booth. Lighted art pieces wil draw the visitor to those pieces.

Don't make it easy for friends and family to stick around for long periods of time. They scare away potential customers. Bring a bar stool or directors chair for you alone. Leave visitor chairs at home.

Have a second person work your booth with you so that one of you can always be in the booth and available to answer visitor questions. This will also discourage theft. Don't bring personal items such as your handbag into the booth. Keep your cash and identification in a fanny pack or art apron pocket.

What to Bring with You

What you will want to bring to your booth are items such as a small cooler with water, snacks, and lunch. Also, if your booth is outdoors, you will want to have a hat and some suntan lotion handy.

As you will always need supplies to hang pictures, have a tool box containing pliers, scissors, screw drivers, hanging hooks, a hammer, 4" and 6" metal spring clamps, 10" nylon cable zip ties, duct tape, pens, pencils, markers, business cards and holder, Windex, paper towels, dust cloth, receipt book, calculator, credit card device, tax chart, order forms, first aid kit, any special equipment needed for lighting, and some small bills and coins for giving change.

In addition, you will want to bring table cloths, folding tables, print racks, chair, a sign-up sheet for people to register for future information about you or shows that you are doing, a sign that says "I take credit cards," and large clear plastic bags in which to put the items purchased. Using large clear plastic bags for packaging up sold paintings can be advertising you as your customer walks around the show.

There are many other items that you may want or need depending upon whether you have your own booth or are sharing with someone else. Every time you do an art show, keep a notebook handy and add to your list as you discover items that you need. It's good to review your list before packing up for every show.

Have appropriate signage. This is fairly obvious, but if you don't have your name displayed, no one will know who you are.

Name Tags

Most artists don't wear a name tag, but it is important to wear one so the visitor recognizes right away that you are the artist. In fact, all people working in your booth should have name tags. Have your name tags professionally made as it will differentiate you from the others.

Pricing Labels

You really need to display the price on each item. Use a title card and put on the artwork title, medium, size, and price. You don't want people to walk away because they can't see the price.

Credit Card Reader

The majority of people don't walk around with a pocket full of cash anymore. That's why it is important for you to take credit cards. It is so easy to set up an account to take credit cards that you don't want to take the chance of losing sales due to not having the ability to process the cards.

There are several companies that furnish card readers that you can attach to your iPhone or Android phones and tablets. These are Squareup.com, PayPal, and Etsy. The percentage rates to these credit card companies are very competitive and there are no monthly fees. You are only charged when you use the reader so even if you only take a credit card now and then, it pays to have the ability to do so.

You may want to have two readers. That way, when your booth is busy, you can use one on your phone and your boothmate can use the one on your tablet.

Or, if for some reason, one doesn't work, you have a backup.

Be sure to place a sign in your booth where it can be easily seen which says that you take credit cards. You can purchase these for very little money and it's smart to display them in several locations in your booth.

Business Cards

Purchasing art is very often an in-the-moment decision and once the visitor walks away, they most often don't come back. Many will ask for or take a business card as a nice way to leave your booth without making a purchase. Give it to them. Business cards are so inexpensive, it is smart to have them available and to give them away. One of those people who took your card may just surprise you and contact you later.

Having a professionally designed and printed card is important. Although I believe it is very important to have your photo on your business card so people will remember you, I also like to see at least one reproduction of your art somewhere on the card. And, why waste the space on the back of the card? Put an image of one of your pieces of artwork there.

Your card should have your name, business name, business address, website, email address, and phone number.

Place your business cards in a holder on the table of your booth where people can easily pick them up.

Also, put about 25 business cards in your right-hand pocket to give out during the day. When you get a card from a prospective buyer, put it in your left-hand pocket so it doesn't get mixed in with the ones you are giving out.

Keep the remainder of your box of business cards in your car, so when you run low, they are close by and not back at the studio in your desk drawer. Also put a colored card in the box about ¾ of the way through the cards so that when you reach that card, you will be reminded it is time to order new cards.

Place a business card in the packaging of every order you sell.

Getting Customers into Your Booth

When people are walking by your booth, smile and speak to them. I know this is a no-brainer, but it is amazing how often I see artists sitting in their booth totally engaged in conversation with each other while spectators aka potential buyers are walking by. It is best to stand during busy times. In this way, you can easily step into the aisle and speak with visitors and steer them into your booth. Having people in your booth will bring more people into your booth. People are curious. They want to see what others are looking at.

Greet all visitors with a statement. It can be as simple as "Welcome to my world," or "Hello." Then engage with your customers.

Develop rapport. The important thing is not what you say, but that you have a warm, pleasant attitude when you say it. Make eye contact and smile. Smiling is important. In the minds of many, art is connected with beauty and happiness. Make sure to wear your positive attitude, even when you are tired or if it is the end of the day. While it is not a secret that you are befriending them only to get their business, being genuinely friendly is more fun, more helpful, and more conducive to long term relationships.

You can ask something along the lines of "What caught your eye?", "What are your favorite colors?", "Do you have a spot in your home for a painting?" "What genre do you like best?" Some of them will want to talk with you, others will not.   If they seem to want to be left alone, say, "Let me know if you have any questions." And then back off a bit.

If you see someone observing a particular painting for a bit of time, start a conversation with them by saying something like, "It's a very powerful painting, isn't it? Would you like to know the story behind it?" Or "What are you seeing in that painting that speaks to you?"

Don't answer a compliment with "Thank You." This psychologically ends the conversation. Say instead that you appreciate the compliment or that you are glad they like it. Add that it is also one of your favorite pieces or ask if they noticed the (item) painted in the background? Say thank you only when they have purchased something.

If the visitor looks at a particular piece of art for a long period of time, tell them a short story about the art piece and how you came to create it. People like to purchase art from someone they feel comfortable with. They want to experience the joy of the purchase. People like art shows because they can connect with the artist which is something they probably won't get to do at a gallery.

Often people are not sure how to approach an artist or what to ask you, so they will ask you something that seems totally off-the-wall to you, but answer the question anyway because it will lead to a conversation and that is why you are there...to have conversation about your art. Conversation leads to sales.

Give Them Something

It is good to have something to give away in order to get people to step into your booth. You can give them something as simple as:

• A card with a picture of your art and your contact information

• Bio sheet with photo of you and your art work that tells your story

• An easy to carry, memorable and hopefully useful piece of swag i.e. a small magnet with your art on it.

Develop Your Fan Base

Collect business cards by having a raffle for a piece of your artwork, preferably a print.

Have a clipboard handy with a place for visitors and customers to sign their names, put their phone numbers and email addresses so you can text or email them about future happenings in which you are participating. Add them to your fan mail base to keep in touch with them whether they buy or not.

Have them text you right there so you can capture their phone numbers and information.

Take a selfie of you with your customers holding the art they bought and send it to them via text or email. Ask them if you can post it on Facebook, Instagram and/or your website.

Then keep in touch with these people by sending them a newsletter, or invitations to other art shows.

"Art enables us to find ourselves
and lose ourselves at the same time."

- Thomas Merton -

Exhibiting In Galleries

Don't randomly call or drop by galleries. Instead, do your homework. Find out a bit about the gallery first. What type of art do they sell? Who do they represent? Why would they be interested in your work? What is the price range of what they are currently showing?

Then when you do call, be prepared with a presentation that tells them why they will be interested in your art. What's the benefit for them? Why would they want to represent you and your work? Have a good arsenal of reasons before you even get in touch with them. Spell out clearly why they should consider showing your work as well as why you want to be represented by them. The more reasons you have, the more likely you are to sell them on representing you.

Before you approach the gallery, make a few personal visits, study the gallery's website and social media pages. Review their exhibition calendar. Make yourself aware of what kinds of artists they represent, read artist statements and show statements. Learn all you can about the gallery's history as well as their policies and procedures for interviewing artists or accepting artist submissions.

Be realistic about how you compare, and make sure you're a reasonable match to the artists they represent before making contact. When you approach a gallery about your art, you need to have a thorough understanding of what they're about as well as why your art and you match up with their existing art, artists, agenda and views.

Always customize your presentation to the gallery you are approaching. Don't use the same approach for more than one gallery. Know the name and title of who you are contacting and what you are going to say about either them or their gallery (or both) to demonstrate that you have clearly done your homework-- and actually care about who they are and what they stand for. Galleries are extremely good at spotting artists who have not done their homework.

Galleries don't randomly select artists who happen to drop by with their portfolio or make contact by email, mail or phone. They don't select artists based on whether they like the artist work or even on how good it is. The quality of your art is important, yes. But there's so much more a gallery is interested in. They select artists based on reputation, experience, accomplishments, and standing in the art community. They also need to know your previous sales history, the quality of critical reviews of your past shows, and very important... what it is like to work with you.

They are looking for the best artists they can find. Someone with marketability. So how do you get recognized as one of these "best artists?"

This may take some time. You'll need to prove yourself by showing your art whenever and wherever you can, building your resume and reputation one step at a time. You need to consistently have successful shows, meaning your work sells well.   It's your job to develop your reputation so that a gallery wants to represent you. You may think that if you have to do all this work yourself, you don't need a gallery. But, you need to understand, if a gallery has a choice between you, with no reputation and low prices on your work, and another artist who has a reputation and higher prices, they will pick the other artist. It is just as much work or maybe even more to represent a new artist with no reputation for less money as it is to represent someone better known. If they are going to put their time into representing someone's work, it only makes sense they will pick someone's work which brings in higher returns. So, it's your job to convince them that it is worth their while to work with you.

Some things you can do to build your reputation are:
- If you're new to the art world, less experienced or don't have much of a resume, stick with galleries near where you live that show mainly new or emerging artists. This will give you a "home field advantage."

- Promote your shows in as many ways as possible including online event calendars, websites that are relevant to your art, social networking pages, blogs, newspapers, and at physical locations where art people tend to congregate.

- Follow any galleries that interest you on social media, and more importantly, "like" and occasionally comment on their posts if you have something genuine and constructive to say and are NOT simply trying to promote yourself. Chances are good that they'll notice you, and maybe even check out your social media pages, profile or website.

- Go on a fact-finding mission, personally visit the gallery. Often you can get a good idea from a visit whether a gallery might be right or appropriate for you. Go to some of their show openings. Look at the art, see how it's labeled, organized and presented. Pick up brochures or any printed materials they have on offer.

"A picture is a poem without words."

– Horace –

Marketing Your Art Online

Some new artists believe if you create art, hungry art lovers will beat down your door to buy it. Unfortunately, that's not true. Your art is competing with millions of others for the time and attention of your potential buyers.

So, you have to become proactive about selling your art. No one will buy your art or know it exists without some hardcore marketing on your part. The good news is that there are plenty of different promotional tactics you can use to build your client base.

More and more art is being sold online every day. As with authors and writers who are skipping the traditional publishing route and are self-publishing, many creative artists are choosing to skip the galleries and the art shows by putting their art online and eliminating the high expense of participating in shows and paying gallery commissions.

Web Site

Every artist who wants to sell his or her work should have a web site. Yes, there are other online sites where you can have a web presence, but those should be in addition to your own website. You will use your website to display your work, give customers a place to learn more about you, have a calendar of events in which you participate, and even show articles that you have written or have been written about you. You can add reviews and link to tv interviews and podcasts where you discuss your art.

A website is a good place for interior designers, galleries, and others who may want to display your art to find you and review your art.

For your website, get the highest quality of digital files of your art as possible. If you don't know how to create these, have someone scan your art that will be uploaded to your site.

You will need a page about the artist with your photo/s and bio.

Your contact information should be above the fold (upper 1/3) on every page of your website.

Be sure to place your art by mediums on your site.

Beside each item, state the size, medium, and other products available with this artwork on it such as prints, cards, cups, t-shirts, trivets, coasters, scarves, etc.

Always keep a copy of all your digital files on your computer.

The best web designer I have found is Jake Naylor. You can contact him at jake@jakenaylor.com or 1 (858) 204-3954

Oh, and use your name in your URL. When looking for you online, people may not know the name of your company, but they will know your name.

Drive Traffic to Your Website

Marketing is about getting your brand out there. You absolutely must be on social media. Don't assume you are being seen because you post on Instagram or Pinterest once a week. With algorithms like they are, very few people actually see your posts. Probably only 2% of your friends list will actually come across your posts. It is imperative that you post a minimum of four to five times a day. I post at 7 am, 11 am, 3 pm, 7 pm, and 11 pm. With posting in different time slots like this, I reach a totally different audience at each time. It certainly doesn't hurt to use the same post more than once. And it is important to post on Facebook, Twitter, Instagram, and Pinterest. If you want to post on all of them and you don't have time to sit down four or five times a day, do it all in one day and schedule the posts. You can use a service such as Hoot Suite to schedule your posts. Or you can hire someone to do it for you. I use Debbie Cohen at DC Social Marketing Group 1 (714) 388-8552. She's very dependable and bills by the minute. So, if it only takes her 14 minutes to do your posts, she doesn't charge you for an hour.

Advertising on Social Media

One of the best ways to get some traffic to your website and sell your art is to use social media advertising. If you're not familiar with the concept, you pay a social media network of your choice to display an advertisement to other users.

Some artists sign up for social media advertising before they truly understand how to get the best results. It's not about how many people see your ad. It's about how many people in your target market see your advertisement.

For example, it's better to have an advertisement that's seen by twenty thousand people who buy your art genre than an advertisement seen by two million readers who don't enjoy that genre. That's because the people who buy your subject matter are more likely to sign up for your mailing list or buy your art than the other readers.

To learn more about your audience, look at your statistics about them. On Facebook and Instagram, these statistics are called Insights. Pinterest and Twitter call this data 'analytics'. Regardless of the name, you need to regularly examine this data and mine it for information you can use to connect with your potential customers.

Using social media sites like Facebook, Twitter, Pinterest or Instagram can be helpful to artists. Linked In is more for business professionals. Unless your art is specifically for leader's offices, Linked In is not the place for you.

Don't think you have to take out a huge ad and spends thousands on your first social media advertisement. It's smart to start by running a few small ads first. This prevents you from wasting money on an ineffective ad and it shows you what your audience responds best to.

Another advantage of starting with small ads is that you can measure your return on investment, so you can learn what to expect from your campaigns. For example, you may find campaigns that run on Wednesday perform better than ads that run over the weekend. This is valuable data, so make sure you're tracking your results.

Whether you're launching a huge advertisement or a tiny one, make sure the ad displays nicely on mobile devices like smartphones and tablets. A smaller device may make your text difficult to read or cut your picture size in half. If you forget to test the ad, it may flop, and you'll be left wondering what happened.

Don't forget that you aren't limited to text and images for your ads. You can create video ads that showcase your products and encourage users to buy. But keep your video short and focused, as most social users won't stick around to watch long videos. Good video ideas could include: a professionally designed art trailer, a quick tutorial related to your niche, a brief Q & A session, or a short behind the scenes segment explaining your inspiration for the art.

Social media advertising really does work. But it can take a few weeks to figure out how to get the best results, so don't give up too soon. Instead, keep setting up ads and tweaking them as you learn more about your client base.

Create a Media Kit

Make it easy for bloggers and reviewers to promote you. Create a special page on your website and name it 'Media Kit' or 'Media'. On this page, include your biography, a professional headshot, a blurb about your art, a high-resolution copy of your art pieces, and the buy link to your art.

Include press releases in your media kit. These can be about your exhibits, your shows, your art, your most recent paintings and yourself. Also send them out to every local newspaper, magazine, tv station and radio station. When the news people are looking for something positive, or something local to put in the news, you want to be the one who has something just waiting in their in baskets.

As your platform grows, you'll need to expand this media kit to include any television reviews, blog interviews, magazine interviews, etc. . But for now, have enough content so promoters can copy and paste to their websites or blogs.

Using Giveaways to Promote Your Art

A great way to promote your art is to use giveaways. You offer participants the chance to win something and in exchange they perform a certain action, like giving you their email address. The advantage of a giveaway is it attracts lots of attention and can really help you grow your platform, if done right. Before you schedule your first contest, here's what you need to keep in mind:

Have a Goal

Be honest about what you want from your giveaway contest. Are you looking to gain more newsletter subscribers? Do you want to gain another 500 likes to your Facebook fan page? Are you hoping for a fresh round of testimonials on Amazon?

Once you know what you want, you can plan your contest around this outcome. For example, if you want 200 more newsletter subscribers, then one of your contest requirements would be joining your mailing list.

Follow the Rules

Each social media platform has special rules for running contests. Facebook doesn't allow you to make liking your Facebook fan page a requirement for entry.

They do this because they don't want people inflating their page with fans that really don't care and are only there for the prize.

However, you can ask your contest participants to like your Facebook page. You just can't use it as a requirement. You also need to clarify that Facebook isn't endorsing or supporting your contest.

Set a Deadline

A contest needs a quick deadline to motivate people to take action. Otherwise, participants decide they'll enter later and they never quite get around to it. That's why you want to run your contest for about a week. Anything longer and you may see a loss of interest.

Choose Your Prizes

It's tempting to giveaway your art as a prize, but don't do this. Your goal is to sell your art. When participants think they have a chance to win your art, they don't buy it. Instead, they enter your contest and hope they're the winner.

However, there are plenty of other items you could giveaway as prizes. You could create promo swag using a site like Zazzle. Using Zazzle, you can create branded journals, pens, canvas totes, mugs, and more.

But you're not limited to print on demand items. You can also choose prizes that relate to the theme of your art. For example, if your art is about royalty in the medieval ages, then a prize could be a small tiara or crown. You may decide the prize is a half-hour consultation or lesson with you or it could be an exclusive code to your insider's club.

Don't throw together a giveaway randomly. Take some time to think through what the rules will be, what prize you'll offer, and how participants can enter to win. Your contest will flow smoothly if you work these details out in advance.

"Curiosity about life
in all of its aspects,
I think,
is still the secret
of great creative people."

- Leo Burnett -

Creating & Building Your Email List

Imagine creating your next piece of art and being able to tell thousands of people who love your work about it. Imagine being able to contact these people anytime you want with news or updates about your art. With your own mailing list, this isn't just a dream. It's entirely possible.

The first thing you need to do to build your email list is choose a mailing list service. There are a few really good options including Constant Contact, Aweber, and Get Response.

Mailing list services charge you by the number of subscribers you have. For a list of 500 subscribers, you can expect to pay $15-25 per month. As your list grows and you get more subscribers, you'll get charged more. However, if you're regularly marketing to your list, then you should easily be able to cover this cost.

If your budget is tight, look into MailChimp. They allow their users to have a free mailing list if you have less than 2,000 subscribers. That means you can build your list for free. Once you have more than two thousand subscribers, you'll have to pay a monthly fee.

Once you've done some research and picked a mailing list company, it's time to get started building your list. Your service provider will give you a special code you can use on your website to add a subscription form.

If you're not familiar with HTML or other coding languages, ask your web designer to put it on your blog for you. Ideally, you need to have your subscription form on the right side of your blog and you need to have it underneath your posts. This makes it easy for your visitors to sign up for your mailing list.

It's smart to offer a free gift to encourage new visitors to sign up for your list. This free gift could be a collection of baseball card sized prints, a calendar, a magnet, or another item with your art illustrated on it. You need something besides a newsletter to entice people to sign up. I don't know one person who wants another newsletter showing up in their inbox.

Now that you have a mailing list and special offer in place, it's time to let the world know. Share about your special gift on social media and invite your followers to sign up for your mailing list.

Don't forget to create a special landing page on your website. This page should mention your free gift and invite visitors to enter their contact information. Once visitors do this, they should immediately be directed to a 'thank you' page.

Now, if you're featured on a webinar or podcast episode, you can tell listeners to head to a specific page on your website in order to sign up for your mailing list and/or your free gift. This can convert more visitors to subscribers, because you're only asking them to do one thing (sign up for your list).

Building an email list of people who love your art is one of the best ways to grow your career as an artist. Experiment with different free gifts to see which one appeals the most to your audience.

"Have no fear of perfection,
you'll never reach it."

- Salvador Dali -

Interacting in Groups & Forums

One simple way to market your art is to interact in groups and forums. This can help drive traffic to your website and boost the visibility of your work. But you don't want to pick just any group or forum to participate in. You want to choose ones that will help you grow your brand.

Participating regularly in groups will also give you lots of ideas. This means you'll have plenty of inspiration to record Facebook Live videos and make blog posts. But the inspiration doesn't stop there. The more you learn about your audience, the easier it will be to target them with your subsequent work.

Along with groups where your buyers hang out, you also want to join groups where you can find fellow artists. Pick places where the mood is upbeat, and artists encourage each other. If you join a group that's negative or thrives on picking people apart, you'll be pulled down by all the negativity.

When you are part of a group, remember to engage in discussions. It can be tempting to parrot what everyone else is saying. But you want to focus on adding value to each conversation. If you regularly share help-ful information and encourage other members, you'll develop a reputation as a trusted leader in your niche.

If forum or group etiquette allows self-promotion, share about your art when joining in conversations. The key here is to only do this when your art is relevant to the topic being discussed.

If you're not sure about the rules of etiquette in the group or forum, take a moment to reach out to the owner or a moderator. This shows you're there be-cause you genuinely care and want to help better this online community.

Build Your Own Group

Leading a group is a great way to show that you're an expert in your niche. But you should only start a group if you're willing to invest time and attention into growing it. At first, you'll spend most of your time mar-keting the group (about 5-10 hours a week).

As the group grows in numbers, you'll start get-ting members who heard about you through word of mouth and want to join in the fun. Pay attention to who is joining your group and remove anyone who attempts to spam your tribe or start flame wars. These are not the type of people you want to be associated with personally or professionally.

Licensing

Many of us see art duplications in retail stores and wonder how those artists got their work duplicated and into the stores. We often think that some of our work is better than those, but we don't know how to go about getting noticed. That work is usually done by independent artists like you and me who are represented by a licensing agent.

A licensing agent is a company that represents you and your work by selling the rights to reproduce your art on specific products for a specific period of time and you receive a percentage of the sales.

Licensing agents work in many different ways. It is important to do your homework and find out exactly what the licensing company will do for you. A licensing agent will sign with an artist for specific types of art such as Christmas or Halloween scenes for popcorn cans or wildlife for puzzles or art that is used on specific items such as fabrics or scarves. If you are an artist with a recognizable style or you have a strong brand, you will possibly be able to attract a licensing company that deals in all kinds of products.

If you would like to pursue this avenue for selling your art, it will require some research on your part. First, you must find out who and where the licensing companies are and then see if your style is a good fit for their company.

Before you get too far into this process, you should probably register your art work with the US Copyright Office. It can save you some headaches further along the line.

Be sure your website is up to date, because that's the first place a licensing agent will look to see what your work looks like.

You really need to do your homework on their company because you want to be able to tell the licensing agent why your work will be a good fit for their products. You must sell yourself and your unique abilities and attributes to them as well as your art.

Once they have indicated an interest in your work, there are many considerations involved in working with a licensing agent.

1. How long have they been in business?
2. How many artists do they represent at any one time?
3. Do the artists they represent specialize in specific categories?
4. What is the split of money?
5. Does the artist also get product?
6. Can the artist buy additional copies of their work? If so, at what discount?

7. What creative services do they offer and what is the charge for these services?
8. What is the length of time the agent will represent you?
9. Will they allow you to speak with any of the artists they currently represent?

There doesn't seem to be any standard agreement in the licensing world. Your agreement with your agent depends on any number of factors from what products your work will appear on to the familiarity of your brand.

Be sure to ask for a copy of the Artist/Agent Agreement. You will want your attorney to advise you as to what legal commitments both parties have in the agreement to ensure you concur.

"We don't make mistakes,
just happy little accidents."

- Bob Ross -

Section 16

Selling to Interior Designers and Decorators

There are literally thousands of interior designers and decorators in the world today and they have an endless need for art. The great thing about these buyers is that they don't care if you are an experienced artist with a name or you are just starting out. They are looking for artwork that goes well with their design aesthetic. And, if they feel your work is what they are looking for, they will probably become repeat customers.

You may not have any idea what a designer is looking for. Half of the time they don't even have any idea of what they are seeking. It's when they see it, they know it is the right piece or pieces. That's why it is important for you to have a number of pieces displayed on your website.

Because designers decorate offices or buildings with lots of wall space, they are often looking for larger pieces of art, 36" x 48" and up. Plus, they are cost conscious because they are looking to make a profit on all the pieces they put into their clients' space.

Therefore, if you have larger pieces of art that you can sell for a reasonable price and still make a profit for yourself, this could be a good market for you. You might also create a series of pieces that can be hung together to fill up wall space and make a powerful statement.

You should always invite the designers in your area to any art shows in which you are participating. Do your homework though. Be sure your style matches their style before reaching out to them. Find out what colors are trending this season, what color palette they are using and what the conceptual inspiration is for their desired design. You will be more successful if your work matches their style and compliments their designs.

Remember, interior designers are people too. Don't be afraid to contact them. They need us. Our art might be the very piece they are looking for. You can find them on Pinterest, Instagram, or Houzz.com. Follow them on social media, send them a note and invite them to a show, send them a digital portfolio or direct them to your website. Pick up the phone, call and offer to stop by their office and show them your work.

You can find interior designers by visiting the American Society of Interior Designers website or by joining the ASID Industry Partners LinkedIn group.

Section 17

A Final Note

When someone buys a piece of your art,

They are buying more than an object.

They are buying hundreds of hours of errors and experimentation, years of frustration, and moments of pure joy.

They are not buying just an item of art.

They are buying a piece of your heart,

A piece of your soul,

A small piece of your life.

Be sure they know the story!

"*Painting is easy
when you don't know how,
but very difficult
when you do.*"

– Edgar Degas –

Resources

Licensing Companies

- American Art Images
- Art Impressions Media Group Inc.
- Artistic Design Group
- Artistic Licensing
- Artists of Kolea
- Art of Possibility Studios (represents physically disabled artists)
- Art Visions
- Artworks! licensing LLC
- Bentley Licensing Group
- Courtney Davis
- Coyote Red Licensing
- CP Licensing
- Creatif Licensing
- Creative Connection Inc.
- Cypress Fine Art Licensing
- DSW Licensing Company
- Fame Farm
- Jewel Branding & Licensing
- JMS Art Licensing,LLC
- Kids-Did-It! (represents children 3-14 years old)
- Licensing Liaison
- Lifestyle Licensing
- Lilla Rogers Studio
- Linda McDonald, Inc.
- Leo Licensing
- London Portfolio
- Looking Good Licensing
- Magnet Reps

- Meehan Design Group
- MHS Licensing
- Mosaic Art Licensing Agency
- Next Day Art
- Northern Promotions, Inc.
- Painted Planet Licensing Group
- Paper Road Art Licensing
- Penny Lane Publishing
- PM Design Group Inc.
- Porterfield's Fine Art Licensing
- Rosenthal Represents
- Ruth Levison Design
- Sagebrush Fine Art
- Sequel Designs and Licensing
- Studio Voltaire
- Suzanne Cruise Creative Services, Inc.
- TSB & Co.
- Two Town Studios
- The Buffalo Works
- Wild Apple Licensing

Sell Art Online

- Artlimes.com
- ArtPal.com
- Art Storefronts.com
- AbsoluteArts.com
- AbstractArtGallery.com
- AdobePortfolio.com
- AffordableBritish Art.com
- Aftcra.com
- AhaLife.com
- AltPick.com
- AmericanHandmade Crafts.com
- ArtAlleys.com
- ArtAttack.com
- ArtBaazar.com
- ArtBoost.com
- ArtClickIreland.com
- ArtCorgi.com
- ArtDex.com
- ArtDiscover.com
- Artebooking.com
- ArtFido.com
- ArtFinder.com
- ArtFire.com
- Artful Home.com
- Artfuly.com
- ArtfullyWalls.com

- Artfully Reimagined.com
- ArtGallery.co.uk
- ArtHit.com
- Articents.com
- Artist.com
- ArtistBe.com
- Artisera.com
- Artistize.com
- Artisouls.com
- ArtistsToWatch.com
- ArtizanMade.com
- ArtLicensing.com
- ArtLicensingShow.com
- Artmajeur.com
- ArtMarketDirect.com
- ArtMuse.com
- ArtofWhere.com
- Artomat.com
- ArtPal.com
- ArtPharmacy.com.au
- ArtPickle.com
- ArtPistl.co.uk
- Artplatform.com
- Artplode.com
- Art Rising.net
- ArtsAdd.com
- ArtShow.com
- ArtSlant.com
- ArtSpan.com
- ArtSpecifier.com
- Artsper.com
- ArtStorefronts.com
- Artsy.net
- ArtsyHome.com
- ArtUrbane.com
- ArtWanted.com
- ArtWeb.com
- ArtworkArchive.com
- Artyah.com
- ArtZyme.com
- AskArt.com
- AxisWeb.org
- Behance.net
- Big Cartel.com
- Bonanza.com
- Brika.com
- CanStockPhoto.com
- CaféPress.com
- Cargoh.com
- Casetify.com
- Chairish.com
- CodaWorx.com
- ColourinYour Life.com.au
- Contrado.com
- CraftisArt.com
- CraftFoxes.com
- Craftersinthebarn.com
- Craigslist.com

- CreativeListings.org
- CreativeMarket.com
- Crevado.com
- CrowdyHouse.com
- Curioos.com
- CustomizedGirl.com
- CustomMade.com
- DailyPainters.com
- DailyPaintWorks.com
- DandelionAlley.co.uk
- Daylighted.com
- DegreeArt.com
- Deviant Art.com
- Displate.com
- DPCPrints.com
- Dunked.com
- Ebay.com
- Ebth.com
- EBSQArt.com
- eCrater.com
- ElectricObjects.com
- Etsy.com
- EyesOnWalls.com
- Facebook.com
- Faire.com
- FineArtAmerica.com
- 500px.com
- FolioLink.com
- Foliotwist.com
- Folksy.com
- Format.com
- FotoMoto.com
- FoundMyself.com
- Gallerizt.com
- GalleryToday.art
- GalleryWorldwide.com
- GLCCraftMall.com
- Global-Art-Exchange.com
- Gooten.com
- GotArtWork.com
- GraphicTide.com
- GreenBoxArt.com
- Greenwich Workshop.com
- GreetingCard Universe.com
- Guidedtheory.com
- Gumroad.com
- HandmadeArtists.com
- Handmadeology.com
- HireAnIllustrater.com
- IamAttitude.com
- Ihirecommercial art.com
- ImageKind.com
- InAFlashLaser.com
- IndieMade.com
- IndieMe.com
- IndieWalls.com

Resources

- InkyGoodnes.com
- InPRNT.com
- Interest Print.com
- IVANZI.com
- JewelSpan.com
- KessinHouse.com
- KingandMcGaw.com
- Kunstmatrix.com
- LaunchMyWear.com
- LokoFoto.com
- MadeByHand Online.com
- Madeit.com.au
- MadeUrban.com
- MakersMarket.us
- Meural.com
- Minted.com
- Miratis.com
- MobilePrints.com
- Modalyst.co
- ModifyWatches.com
- MossPiglet.co.uk
- MyBestCanvas.com
- MySoti.com
- MyStudioAssistant.com
- Neogradys.com
- NewEraPortfolio.com
- NewBloodArt.com
- NotOnTheHigh Street.com
- OffTheEasel.com
- OpenSky.com
- Original-Art-Under 100.com
- Our-wv.com
- Patreon.com
- Personalise.com
- RedBubble.com
- RiseArt.com
- SaatchiArt.com
- SableAndOx.co.uk
- SculptSite.com
- See.me
- Shapeways.com
- SignedCards.com
- ShopHandmade.com
- Shopify.com
- ShowFlipper.com
- Showyourarts.com
- SiOTTGallery.com
- SmugMug.com
- Society6.com
- Soldsie.com
- Spoonflower.com
- Spreadshirt.com
- Spreesy.com
- StateOfTheArt Gallery.org
- StoreEnvy.com
- SwiftGalleries.com

- Teespring.com
- TheCommissioned.com
- TheCraftersBarn.co.uk
- TheDiscerner.com
- TheFunkyArt Gallery.com
- TheMatBoard.com
- ThePlace4Art.co.uk
- ThisIsALimited Edition.com
- Threadless.com
- TopHatter.com
- Touchtalent.com
- Treniq.com
- TurningArt.com
- Ugallery.com
- UncommonGoods.com
- Vida.com
- Wanelo.com
- WolfandBadger.com
- WowThankYou.co.uk
- XanaduGallery.com
- YayPrint.com
- Yessy.com
- Zatista.com
- Zazzle.com
- Zenya.com
- Zet.gallery
- Zibbet.com

Art Podcasters

Abbi Jacobson
A Piece of Work
ajacobson@wnyc.org
www.wnycstudios.org/shows/pieceofwork

Cory Huff
The Abundant Artist
coryhuff@gmail.com
www.theabundantartist.com

Leslie Saeta
Artists Helping Artists
lsaeta@gogle.com
artistshelpingartistsblog.blogpot.com

Duncan MacKenzie
Bad At Sports
duncan@badatsports.com
www.badatsports.com

Danielle Krysa
The Jealous Curator
danielle@thejealouscurator.com
www.thejealouscurator.com

Tamar Avishai
The Lonely Palette
lan.elsner@gmail.com
www.thelonelypalette.com

Mike Montgomery/BenUyeda
The Modern Maker Podcast
make@mikemonty.net
info@homemade-modern.com
www.modernmakerpodcast.com

Tyler Green
The Modern Art Notes Podcast
tylergreendc@yahoo.com
www.manpodcast.com

Antrese Wood
Savvy Painter Podcast
antree@antrese.com
www.antrese.com

Life Affirming Resources by Judi Moreo

Judi Moreo is an internationally acclaimed speaker, author, and coach. For over twenty years, Judi has studied the lives and habits of highly motivated and successful people. She has unraveled the mystery behind the illusion that only a chosen few are allowed success and has become a respected authority on high level performance, personal development, and self-esteem.

Her unique approach to helping people succeed has made her one of the most sought-after keynote speakers in the nation. You can now take advantage of her knowledge and expertise through her books.

You may order the following books online at: www.judimoreo.com/shop

You Are More Than Enough: Every Woman's Guide to Purpose, Passion & Power

This is a powerful guide to discovering your purpose, unleashing your passion, and changing your habits to realize the success you want in all the areas of your life ---personal and professional relationships, career, finances, and security.

The Achievement Journal

This is a life changing tool. It is a method for organizing goals, dreams, and expectations -- as well as evaluating what's working, what's missing, and what's needed to bring positive results into your life.

Fast Track to Writing and Launching Your Book

Writing and publishing a book can give you huge exposure and help you establish expertise and authority in your market when done right. Planning is the key and that's exactly what this book will help you do every step of the way. When you have a plan in place for how you'll write, publish and market your book, the process is much more enjoyable and achievable.

Overcoming Cancer: A Journey of Faith

Through her personal story, inspiring quotes and practical suggestions, Judi shows us that cancer and fear are messages to us to make lifestyle changes. This supportive book can help the newly diagnosed cancer patient ask better questions, understand there are alternative and integrated treatments that can work and, most of all, maintain hope.

Choices Magazine
Choices is an international online quarterly magazine designed to encourage you to make the right choices and live successful lives. If you have ever felt that you were created for "something more," but just didn't know what or where to start, this publication is for you. It features articles on ways to make your life work. Sign up to receive your complimentary subscription. www.judimoreo.com

The World of Creativity television show
Judi Moreo is the host of *The World of Creativity*. If you are an artist or an author and you would like to be interviewed on this popular show, contact Judi at (702) 2833-4567 and find out how you can make it happen.

Turn Your Art Into Cash Order Form

To order additional copies of this book for $19.95 each + shipping/handling, please complete the form below.

Email orders: judi@judimoreo.com

Telephone orders: +1-702-283-4567
Please have your credit card ready.

Postal orders: Turning Point International
3315 E. Russell Road, Ste. A4-404
Las Vegas, Nevada 89120
USA

See our website www.judimoreo.com for FREE information on:
Other books, *Choices* magazine, Speaking/Seminars, Consulting

Name: ____

Address: ____

City: ____

State/Province: _______________________ Postal Code: ___________

Telephone: ____

Email: ____

Sales Tax: ____________

Shipping by air: ______________

Payment Type: ☐ Check   ☐ Credit Card (Visa, MasterCard, AMEX)

Card Number: ____

Name on Card: ____

Expiration Date: ________ / ________   Billing Zip Code: ____________